IN THE DRINK

EMILY CROCKER

First published 2021
by Subbed In

© Emily Crocker 2021

Book and cover design by Dan Hogan
Text set in 8pt Domaine Text

First edition

Printed and bound in Birraranga (Melbourne)

National Library of Australia Cataloguing-in-Publication:
Crocker, Emily
In The Drink / Emily Crocker
ISBN: 978-0-6451524-5-6 (paperback)

Subbed In 012

All rights reserved.

This book is copyright. Apart from any fair dealing for the
purposes of research, criticism, study, review or otherwise
permitted under the Copyright Act, no part of this book may be
reproduced by any process without permission. Inquiries should
be addressed to Subbed In: hello@subbed.in

www.subbed.in

These poems were written and edited on the stolen land and waterways of the Wadi Wadi people of Dharawal Country, and the Cadigal-Wangal people of the Eora Nation. This book was printed and bound on the stolen lands of the Woiwurrung (Wurundjeri) and Boon Wurrung people of the Kulin Nation. Sovereignty was never ceded. Emily Crocker and Subbed In pay their respects to elders, past and present.

Always was, always will be Aboriginal land.

Contents

8	Stamps for concession cardholders
10	Marsh
12	Soda water, vodka and essential oils of your choice
14	Watermelon pips, swallowed
16	Wok over high heat
18	Imitation plants
20	$1 coffee
22	Sacred as mud
24	Confession
26	Fats and oils
28	Onions
30	Wishbone
32	Astronaut
34	Spooks
36	In your sleep you spoke of utopia
38	⅓ cup of soil
40	Union of two
44	The Tower
48	Happy Birthday
50	17:27 to Lithgow
54	Our lungs so full
58	Watching the grass grow
64	The dead cannot die

66	Compost
68	Dash
70	Soon
72	Keep your receipts
74	Never strikes twice
76	Multicoloured cereal
82	Sausage meat
84	Brood
86	Landscaping for the masses
88	Just add water

Stamps for concession cardholders

Nearly in the drink,   we are trying
to wash each other's   feet without touching.
mardi gras weekend   and the last before
you leave. How I can't blame you for all
the trash in sydney.   Tent pitched; the pegs slid
easy into sand   and the sun melting
into the nuttelex   horizon. I smile
secretly, O'Hara-style, at the sheer
inevitable picnic of our lives if we could
just sit still. For once. Pretending
to relish the coarse   plants growing out of
the naked dunes. Eyes   down, pull through strands
and noose my finger   tips.   You slip away
                                    in the humidity
like the label from   a bottle of draught,
as you list all the   things I want for you
too.   Things you could drop
                              behind the microwave
Or jam under   wobbly tables.
A bottle-opener   worn down to the gums.
Business cards stuffed into empty parts
of both our futures.   Sometimes you have to
believe a postage stamp   could tear a hole
in the side of your sharehouse. Lest you
suffocate under relentless   hoping.
The type you   must rip back
from your unshaved knee in

                                        one

quick motion.

Marsh

The stink of ocean swings into the doorway
of this old wet terrace. A milkcrate of seaweed
gleaned from the beachier side of town swelling
in the cold fresh rain. I hear it makes good mulch
and that gardening keeps the anxiety back. 'These times
are a matter of preference – usually considered
ready when the root is the length of the seed' says
the canadian zine about sprouting and magick.
The potatoes, desperate to see in the dark, silently
explore the corners of the green bag under the sink.
With their mauve fingers and keen sense of smell
they can taste right through the particle board
to the marsh this place is. Apparently, when poor people
could still afford to live here, there was
an Agent Orange factory upstream. Friends urge us
to test the soil before we plant anything to eat.
But I'm trying to grow my way out of the habit
of pocketing knots of ginger at the supermarket,
or the occasional slender bouquet of broccolini
eased from the rubber band. You've swam
in that same harbour all your life.
And so far, so good.

Soda water, vodka and essential oils of your choice

Bring you back to house number four in ten months
where the bathroom smells like cat litter crystals.
And I won't mention all my hair
clogging the shower drain. The menthol
tiles are rubbery when wet, and I have been
waiting for a secure landing. Fingering
the chipped corner of the mirror
I recall how tense optimism can be
continually applying ourselves to it
like a free sample of department store moisturiser.
I will never know if mouthwash tastes
the same to you as it does to me, only
that there is such a thing as the tasting.
When I put a spare toothbrush in the medicine cabinet
I wanted our mouths to taste the same.
That even as my skin foams, fissures and collects
an unremarkable grey in the crevices, if you
pried me open, I'd be milky underneath.
And you'd still call. Drop by sometime and give me
a home haircut. The clippers spitting along the latex
of my skull. Shards of follicles flickering
like confetti across the tiles.

Watermelon pips, swallowed

Then, the bottom shelves in the pantries of our childhood homes
choked with tins of fruit. $10 per kilo for bananas
was just the start of it. *Don't you put those pineapple rings
on your burger, kids. We're going to need them
when they turn the produce freezers off. We're going
to need them if your father* swallows all that bait

Today, I hack the rind off a watermelon while she showers.
Fucked and still hungry, we suck at the chunks and tongue
fibers from the back of our teeth, sweating into the couch
in front of Shark Tank. She says fruit is so sexy
as a drop of bland juice runs into her ugly navel.

A friend asks if we were made this way as an act
of artificial selection. Everyone I have ever loved
is insatiably frugal. Unoccupied arms bred to tie off
and bring in the broken nets for mending. One darns
socks with strips of her dead grandmother's hosiery,

oyster-coloured stockings. A type I would never wear.
Why buy new ones when the world could end tomorrow?
Even if aldi has father's day specials this catalogue-week.
Tell me what garden tools have to do with fatherhood?
What good is the plant for eating once it has gone to seed?

The women in front of us at the checkout, always look
so famished as they stock up for the whole brood, uncle tobys
and heart-smart mincemeat. Nod anxiously at our trolley-load
of canned beans.
Our attempt at the good life. Back home we tear the clingwrap
from the zucchinis before any house guest can see.

Wok over high heat

Charcoal crumbles out of his jaw.
My hands are shamefaced from cutting chillies.
Pat a reserved palm on the collar of his jersey.
One, two. One, two.
One eye on the saucepan of rice.
Two limbs taken up by
folding.

The news still muttering on the television
blunders into the cricket, pretending to not see
the mess boiling over
in the nation's living rooms.

We wobble, aspic in the chill
of the draft saucing the floorboards.
The trial and error of having a body.
Congealing until none of the skin fits.
Grows damp, sticks and stretches
under his weight. Sloughs off like a marinade.

When the sobbing stops, and he goes to shower,
I sweep up the ash from the dining room floor
and pocket it away.

Imitation plants

Having missed the last bus, we wound up
alongside a pile of broken furniture
left al fresco for council collections
dowels bursting accusations
from chipboard pieces.
        Tactical-vomiting green foam
the strings of plastic foliage
stripped from your stomach lining
slopped on the nature strip
don't look as Fresh! as they would've
year in year out.
        There are care instructions inside your jacket.
I start wiping you clean with a dry cloth.
You come away smeared but
it doesn't look too bad in the low light
I missed the secrets, passed matrilineally,
of how to put your ugly away
how to get the sticky out of the dry carpet
of your retching throat.
        A window shudders open and a woman calls from the
        ground floor

> *they just don't make things*
> *like they used to.*

The matriarch had coral in her spine and three
broken dining chairs marooned on the front lawn –
a wilted reef sitting down to an overpriced cafe
breakfast after being evicted from the kitchen.
The hole in her nape squeezes the air like a zit.
Squeamishness is a pinch in the gullet, a mouth bleached.
    They don't use coral no more, either
                            (maybe it was clear off, go'n
                              get out of here)

$1 coffee

The tomato sauce tang of petrol smells vagrant.
A man tickled rouge by stanley's finest
shiraz cab matured in cardboard with pink
pig bladders for ankles rolls in belly up.
Number 5 an' a packet of Winnireds, luv.
Gelatinous eyeing the girl at the counter
like a sausage roll behind a sliding door
of insulation-glass. A young bloke in
Sydney-clothes catches the sweaty back hand
of the look. He clenches his knees
glaring at the juice fridge where
all of the packaging thinks it's cooler than it is.

Sacred as mud

You have found yourself nodding through charcoal chicken surplus. You, budget-hotel icon. Post-renovation and unsure how to define cannibalism with PR in mind. The cabbies are swapping shifts. Beaky arts school kids roll skinny durries on the bench where the homeless guys used to sit. We are pecking through the skip in a quiet fumble. Upon milk crate and short-sighted. There are a dozen bags of bread. We take the sourdough ones and a sweaty pillow of salad leaves.

    Once, while drinking in the park, we saw an environment and heritage deployment wrestle you into a bag for tagging. A French tourist approached to ask *What will you do now? Eat him?*

    Now, a woman emerges from the glass auto-doors with a translucent grey bag of frozen prawns. 'Oh! What a beautiful bird!' Her accent tastes like capers. You keep juggling the chicken bone between your elegant features. We're all caught under the omnipotent glow of the liquorland sign.

Confession

After seeing the truth squeezed murky and thin
from a dish cloth   take a pill
to delay emotions.   The undersides
of fingers pushed   to breast.
The thread feels   swollen and numb
on the face of one button   clumsily replaced
on the linen blouse blushing at the cuffs.
Perhaps, where the wash bled.   Or the beets.
Things bleed.   It's fine as long as it stops.
The lighting of candles   if you'll just hang on
a moment for the match to take   like a transfusion.
The details matter.   Conversation is a surgery.
Practiced. Revising   every bend   to wash hands
for the meal   and smoothing down shirtfront
again   like a tablecloth. Before it's said
in one ladle-full.   The bowl of the serving spoon
          a pendulum.   Leaves a burst
of tomato   a red lake between us.
Even once the plates are cleared
and the vinyl top   wiped down.   And re-wiped
from lunch crumbs or craft projects.
An orange border remains   caution tape
to be spoken around.

Fats and oils

Having passed ziplock bags of brazil nuts through
    the self-serve checkout
    as banana chips
  the brittle bullets of their bodies
  sit fat in the pouches of my face.
I remember you telling
how years of energy goes
into one rich seed. We pictured oily
embryos boiling in the cheeks of shells
drooping from optimistic trees.
    Each time I pull a jacket over
      the muscles
        butterflied on my back
    I am wearing a butchery display cabinet
    cold and transparent with thick shine.
At business, I reek of glass cleaner.
All day handle myself with plastic bags
bunched over my fists.
And I don't even eat meat. Just push
and prod myself around the bottom
of a freezer-safe container.
    Saying that next year
next year won't be like this.

Onions

When I masturbate I think about buying onions.
A kilo of dry brown shoulders rolling
over each other in the net.
I think about birthday wishes I haven't sent.
Whether I can afford haloumi this week.
The salty shells of pistachios. Thirsty jaws
scraping the colour off my nails.
I wonder if I should get my eyes tested.
Go to the dentist. Remember that time
I asked for a pap smear and the doctor
wanted to talk about my mood instead.
Unanswered emails kneel on me. The hair
in the bathroom sink chokes me. The overflowing
wastepaper puts its hand over my mouth.
As the lawnmower next door grinds towards
the edge of the fence and a chorus
of sandpaper rises in my skull.
I can't believe there is still grass out there
pushing its sick fingers down my throat
and curling into my larynx. Beckoning
for me to forget the breadcrumbs in my sheets,
the torn flyscreen, the internet bill on the fridge,
the need to please.

Wishbone

Taking your hip bones from the countertop
I wish to clothe you from the linen cupboard.
Organic bamboo.　　Modern greys.　　　　The good stuff.
Wipe the purple jewels of dishwater guts
from your wrists.　　The watery blood
from your brow.　　My cheek an absorbent pad
against the exposed flesh of yours.
We hold the plastic tray of the kitchen floor　　　　still.
Until the oven timer cracks us　　　　　　　in two.

I wrap the smaller part in a serviette and place it under
the lip of a plate.

The larger　　　　I let you keep for good luck.
You bring it, between tongs,　　　　　　to your teeth and say
　　　　　　　　　　　　the marrow tastes like an ending.

Astronaut

You keep going on dates with men with an unread copy of Infinite Jest and identical collections of wacky socks because that girl at the women's library told you you'd meet a Virgo. They all turn out to be Aquarius. Or worse, Geminis. You tell me that when you were a kid you wanted to be an astronaut. I sit on your bed in your boxers and your hockey jersey, reading Anne Carson aloud. Your sister taps on the thin wall between the bedrooms. We look at each other. I close the book. After turning out the lamp, you say you like the way I talk about sex. As if I was making a meal. I don't answer because your sister is trying to sleep. Holding myself still against the whoosh of time, I listen to your enjambed breathing up against the wall. All night my thoughts rehearse stories around my watch. The face looking in from the bedside table as if I were a lover.

Spooks

I, a ghost of myself (groans and all), and you, cumbersome
with so much opacity. Itching in the aisles of hangers.
Each point of contact enacting a five-star violence
they don't know to call a violence; grinning and belted.
Glitching in the aisles,   mate   ah   ma'am.
I knew I was a wo~~rry~~man when I began using my form
as a floatation device,   a skeleton key,   a dustpan –
corrections in neat brushwork v, v, v, v, v   v, v, v, v, v
I knew you were really alive each time your body
ingested the words   a lie, a lie, a lie,   like
snips of red felt by the traitor   ah,   *tailor*
placing pins in the lack of it all. Grief is a puncture in the lobe
that never quite closes – a moaning *o,*   *o,*   *o,*   *o*
How desirous you are, at times,
to slip inside a different mass   like a lapel pin,
if it could only hold you close   ah *closed*   ah *clothed*.
All the while I am holding my~~breath~~self open
where I have nothing for you.   Which is to say, so much
                                longing
it haunts us both. Undress yourself and slip inside my body,
elusive as it is, anytime you want to.

In your sleep you spoke of utopia

I saw you an oozing tear on the linen
peeking through the wound in our rest
and it was revolutionary simply because
you gave yourself permission to feel it.
You who are young enough still that all
we have in this world are our bodies,
racing depreciation to make more of it.
Who squeeze the ineffable from bruised
vegetables   the sticky material of the words
melting like chocolate coins in our fist
as we seize the means of reproduction.
Who reaches for my hand in public places
like you know   they'll come for the singers first
for our dirty talk   the names I enter you with
defy history reassemble your organs while
the pulse keeps beating.   Call me
the most offensive sour-milk carton that's ever
slammed into you from a passing car
and watch the curds become beautiful
globing like lace curtains on our skins
and carry on dipping your black-market biscuits
and buzz-cutting your hair among our dappled friends
and our dead heroes.
Carry on stroking the hard air as it swells
with blood and I will take everything you could be
into my mouth and suck on your hopes
until they detonate on the steps of The Department
(whichever spited us most recently).
How you will allow yourself to feel
every roll of my gullet and yell a riot
while we unified by desire pull each other off
course into bodies of survival into
something to live for

⅓ cup of soil

At dinner, christmas beetles going
straight for the butter, I remind a friend
that sometimes taking care of your own
means estranging yourself. Someone passes
an oversized jalapeno jar refilled with gin,
soda stream, lemons from the tree and mystery
syrup we found in the fridge — quince, maybe
just   because
    you're   poor
doesn't mean   you have to
                       hate yourself
could
      die tomorrow
                       you know
we are each in our own way a green frond
trembling. I know there is no response
ready at your fingertips to be pulled
moist and new from the ground.
We don't want to accept that we could be
sad because someone who we've never met
was made sad a long, long time ago. Even though
scientists have grown a date palm from
a 2000-year-old seed found during archaeological
excavations. We still ask each other
                how are you?
The asking itself is a kind of answer.
An admission to the sublime uncertainty
crowding into a film camera frame.
Collectively squinting into the burning coil
of a setting sun. I am holding all the things
I'd do different and can still think
I'd rest happy if this was the last thing I ever saw.

Union of two

Survey cast back the day after
the forms arrived despite invites to wait
drink wine and tick boxes together
like a family.
The envelope sailed through the confidential slit
– big and red with its own authority.
Felt it fall   the whole

                        course

                                  down

my   oesophagus and
                                thud
somewhere deep in the hollow. Hesitating
before the cast iron lips of the post box,
I was slapped by the want
to mutter a private chant.
Inherited faithful rhythm rose
and balleditselfup in my throat
struggling to forgive
those who have trespassed against us
and the sleight that a seat at the reception
could fill the cavity
left by democracy.

Ten months later,
        the sequins
on your wedding dress
        hang   like suns,
as the buttons on your bride's jacket
catch fire.
From my seat I am
pried   open;
a coin tin
        glinting
in the new day.
My sternum   floating
like all the plastic bottles

in the bay
after a week of rain.
The celebrant says 'the union
of two people'
and pauses
for the cheer while you
hold there, among the trees,
like a family.
And it's the lunar standstill
through the vows
where my bitterness shifts
on its axis   into freshwater grief
and I quietly net and pull out
the hopes I still cling to
surfacing from the deep
of my drunk and angry
party mouth
wanting our money's worth
for all the trouble.
As if you can return
permission
you never asked for
and keep
the glimmering rest of it.

The Tower

precarity
is the damage
done to knees
after eight hours
               coiled
on a back seat
a t-shirt wedged in the cracked window
a can of mosquito repellent   last month
     you scrapped the first car you ever owned
one less engine sharing the troposphere
$250 cash in hand   and faith
     that you'll keep this roof over their heads
for at least another rattle   around
the anthropocene of   not knowing
     what to say to the dying houseplants
     greywater falling through their soily sieves
     leaking across the lino

•

put down the tower of rooms you carry
     summit to summit like a boulder
home is a leaking cup   never filling but can be
     sheltered in when everything turns up
somewhere to go on clapping   like a tongue
around the hand scoop of empty   where
we once thought they watched over us
     but looked up to see the slow wink
          of cameras and
construction cranes

•

a summer worked in an office so air conditioned
you had to hold   a mug of repeatedly boiled water
to bend your fingers far enough   to type and
were shot awake   forehead smacking
                            in
                            to
                            the   desk

no one else seemed to feel
the agonising chill so you   said nothing
                                        as they debated
                            the cost of hostile architecture
        to *deter* the homeless guy who had taken to sleeping
    in the thin arch of doorway and reading the newspapers
                            (*can you believe it?*)
                            you gave your two weeks and felt
                            untouchable
months later this employer was
listed on the rental application form

                        I guess they didn't bother to call

                            •

            out the window the oil heater
reappears on the street   a few doors down
                            in the kitchen damp rises
        grease settles   squeezing the cabinets
at each end until the hinges   pop   open
                the trick is to not finish up the last
sucker standing on the lease   when the roof caves in

                surrounded by possums
                        abandoned things
                        of housemates past
                a thousand cables for absent devices
for now you make a monstera leaf   with   your   fingers
say I am scared of being the last generation
left to clean out the shut off refrigerators
exhaling mouldy grief into the world at large
as it curls   an ingrown nail
                        deeper
                        into itself

Happy Birthday

It induces such an appetite   for ribs
to know I was the first person to call you   honestly.
The names you've tried on collecting in my cheeks
like bar mix. The woody aftertaste   carried over
to two burnt matches   suspended   in the air conditioning
with our feet up on the vinyl seats   of the last
train south.   Caught it by a whisker
running   through the stench of cement   away from another
obligated goodbye.   Elope with me.
It's another way of saying your name is a birthday cake
never ordered.   No other option
but to eat your way out.   While the walls are on fire.
In that trendy bar.   And everyone is singing.
Singing by name.   And patting you   on the eggshell
with a countertop. Whites frothing forth over clear liquor.
Now,   all stations.   My palate is filling with paper serviettes
and the violet blooms of cracked pens. There is too much to say
the words smudge across the fleshy triangle   of my hand.
Navy motion draining into my stomach   straight off the sloping
                        window.
Staring back across the grey opening of the carriage floor
the woolly unspoken fills my ears with nausea   and pops
                              in a minty bubble.
To be fair,   we weren't intended   to be commuted this way.

17:27 to Lithgow

Settled in, with her slip-on walking shoes perched
on the footrest, having just poured an instant
cappuccino sachet into a thermos of steam
the woman across the aisle is eating a single-serve
banana bread from the station kiosk and doing
the cryptic crossword in the herald.

    Reading glasses slipping on her slender beak. Plastic
fork, with its patient lean, speared into the glossy surface of the
cake when she picks up her pencil after pulling

        'happy with what's inside? (7)'
                or
        'woody plant with opposite tastes (11)'

out of the flickering
landscape.   The letters stamped into the rock
as the train shoots through the passage blown
into the terrain.

    I think of my mother travelling alone for the first time
in 30 years, up through the red core of this continent. Eating
weet-bix in her hotel room but sparing none on a scenic flight
over Kakadu. Even though she is so afraid of flying she did not
return to home's cool kiss for her own mother's funeral. And I
promise myself to call
        as soon as I get off.

    Even if just to hear her oddly stern voicemail recording
and be told, whenever she rings back, deciphered from a
message-to-text, that she's sorry she missed it.

    That she was having too much fun eating fritters
    in an organic market,
    or watching the display
    at a local history museum.
    That I won't believe it, they have goggles
    with a video in it that goes all the way around the room.

The woman has finished half of her banana bread.
Uncrumples the clingwrap and closes
it around the remaining piece. Reading glasses
now folded on the newspaper in her lap.
She is stumped by 16-down and bored of it
and looks a treat   in the dappled light
                                        drumming through the window

Doesn't smile when she catches me watching.
Instead exhales and returns her conserved attention
to the outside frothing by.

Our lungs so full

Waiting on the grey plastic chair
the way water waits on oil, I google
a translation of the latin embroidered
on the cop's shoulder. 'Punishment will
follow guilt quickly'. Grief is a history
I have much yet to learn. Two bronze envelopes
pass through the gap in the window
between the back of the copshop
and the rest of the world. Both sporting
bright orange BIOHAZARD stickers.
The cop squeezes a bunch of blue nitrile gloves
through the same gap. The gloves bloom hydrangea
from the bulge in my jacket pocket, pressing out
like a throat lozenge from a foil tray
into the eruption of darlinghurst road.

The night after the death I go
to see a friend read poems at my old haunt
and feel like a ghost. A leak in the wall.
Every last open-micer is repeating the line
it comes in waves and the tense cliché
of my own breath exhausts me. Gasps
like the skinny cushion on the floor of a punk bar
full of strangers who all know your name but
all of a sudden know nothing about you.
The green of your carefully tended plot
where all the characters ~~are punished in a rising sea~~ die.   In waves.   And then what?
What of all the hours driving around stealing milkcrates
to make into tables and stools. What of all the cable ties
lovingly looped between each other so we'll feel
the tug in the dark when another slips
                      from the net.

Somewhere unseen, they syphoned a sterile excuse for air
through his lungs. Not a single spore or pollen
until they removed the tubes.
And then there was nothing.
Thank god, there was nothing.
That whole week I revived the poems that drowned
in his mind, disinfectant rising like a tide, face down
on the hospital floor. And in the end, it isn't even
astonishing that I let the same dead men
writing to a silenced landscape
haunt the obituaries,
name each ash
in wheezy recitation.
Outside, the rest of the world continued, usual business,
        to burn.

To love is to open yourself up to loss. Our lungs
so full of love, no wonder sometimes we can't breathe.
I wake at 4am and place my ear beside my lover's nostrils.
Listen to their cilia grating love through the open window just
to check I actually woke up and that it is in fact love in my lungs,
or at least panic, and not industrial disease. Drive one love the
5 minutes home after the gig so she won't have to walk her love
past the house of boys who spat on another of our loves. We
set the car air to recirculate, the gas molecules clothes-swap
between themselves and we suffocate a little more. When
there is no funeral, another love sends poppies
to the house I'm staying at, and hay fever, or perhaps the
agrochemicals, burn my eyes my ears my sinuses out and this
too is love because what is love in this hellscape if not agitation
the bloomex card reading *you, my love, when it gets too much,
I'll see you in the streets*
and it is already too much.

Watching the grass grow

1.

your old man would say if you want to see
the danger coming when it comes keep the grass
clipped short in the open-cut cul-de-sac
the same one he would come home to
at seven-thirty-am and so exhausted once
he pulled up at a house he'd never seen before
and in that moment with Radiohead
on the stereo was stuck in the Schrodinger's box
of anywhere and nowhere the benevolent
neglect of empty terracotta pots perched
in the standard family portrait pose cat belly-down
between the wheelie bins as good as dead
he circled the mitsubishi all the way
down one dead-end and all the way back
into another clutched like a pair of pearls
to the breast of the suburb trying to retrace
his way while the whole of the outdoors
pretended to be a cluedo playing board

2.

lawn coming from *launde* meaning *barren*
as in crops everywhere and nothing to eat
as in specified leisure area as in
the cricket green nearly made it
onto the coat of arms as in fiercely
tending the alien weed the galaxy
of stubborn tentacles silently sucking
away at the country turning the satellite
view on googlemaps into strike paper
interrupted by the occasional pinky-nail of backyard blue
as in your grass's looking a bit crisp mate
tumbling over the colourbond like a mrs mac
cheese and bacon pie bag parachuting
on the crinkly wind as in whose plants
are brown and thirsty now

3.

better to ask for forgiveness than to
carry on worrying about the rent market
so we pull up all the sheets of astroturf
in our mostly cement backyard looked down upon
by 300-degrees of this-decade apartment blocks
and build raised garden beds out of pallets
stolen from the back of Unanderra warehouses
filled them in with free soil from a swimming pool
excavation in Gwyneville it's all croquet anyway
our desire to truly stabilise the dirty
pit in the belly of the planet and how
we are each in our inability to do so
a desperate green blade cold from the ground
at the end of the day our rhizomatic
family took (like a set of organs) to the veranda
to admire our handy work and hope for rain

4.

it was Todd on the nature strip with a bare fist
the legend goes 2007 and a grandfather dead
among the agapanthus the first fatality
over hosing – did he see it coming for him
in this terrible new century over the short
back and sides? the turf species once
reserved for up north creeping into
southern suburbs and then golden-blonde
monocrops bleached in the relentless sun
to be mowed down in the ever closer shave
between exclusive and extinct

The dead cannot die

but still, every night, he is raising the pistol
he never owned. The one
that sprays white noise everywhere.
My only job is to keep
pushing back the bodies
of the children, like paper boats,
as they run in from the driveway.
Send them back to their homes.
It's dinner time.
The streetlights are coming on.
And then I search the car.
It is full of pages, blank.
And I must push myself back out into the driveway.
From there I watch as, again, he raises his arm.
I run to him but I am running through stormwater.

Compost

Like emptied prayer flags, anaemic and unanswered,
damp tea bags flap cold on the line, retrieved.
Re-ingesting discarded parts of myself by the mugful,
the compost bin hunched in a colourbond corner,
its belly full of hair clippings and coffee grounds.
Ambiguous packaging, polyvinyl clinging to itself.
When I mulch my body in this metaphor I am
by the dirt implicated as both garden and gardener.
Produce has the metallic tang of blood.
The smell on your hands after counting money.
Polymer banknotes chapping against each other
with the soft rhythm of a spade. Is that why we stress
the O when we speak of apples? To not muddle
fruit and fruit. A stinking breeze haunts
my mornings. We howl together. A stressed
O O Over the garbage truck beeping and spluttering.
I mourn the space I take up. Eat my words
down to the last scrape every time. Suspend
the plastic things like baubles from the hills hoist.
A grim orchard blooming.

Dash

The refinery lolls
lighting up the headland
like a dashboard, sky vacant.
Quarter moon sticking
powdered aluminium
to your ears, your neck.
Leaves a shadow mask
around the cups of your cheeks.
Scurrying out to pay
for petrol under
the cheese-flavoured orange glow.
164.11 per litre for E10
but you've been driving
with the fuel light on all month.
The price at the pump
creeping up while
this whole wheezing city
runs on empty.

Soon

It is a sweaty October night and
the jacaranda are already bowing.
Overworked mothers
mop at the watercoloured pavement.
Purple at first.
Then the brown clots of too many
too soon.
I am terrified of becoming
the jacaranda. So
take my guilt into your mouth
like a washed pebble.
A past lover
accused me of ovulating
whenever I felt empty.
To be fertile today is to
carry loss inside us,
a crowning blind spot.
Your palm perspires an avalanche
down my neck.
Every day we are edging
into each other's ears
saying too little too late.

Keep your receipts

Sacrifice your empty bottles
           to the milkcrate
           beside the back door.

Keep your receipts.
           So when they come to collect
           your shoes from the back step
you can claim back your charity.
           The coins you didn't condescend
           to re-pocket.

10c per container is cute. But
           you've got an SUV now
           and headphones that shut out
the kids playing in the carpark.
           Oil spilt into hideous rainbows
           and paddlepops melting
                       outside the servo.

The velvet petrol fumes salivate
           but the world we know is
                       dripping
                       away.

Never strikes twice

Power outlet entombed mid-melt
prongs curling into
prop vampire teeth.
Keeps it on the kitchen windowsill
beside the dish brush and sink plug.
The fluid from the helicopter
laying its body of
        molecules
over the remorseless fire
made the most   incredible   sound.
Rebuilt the flat himself out of
the black. In careful stretches
        of autumn mornings bending
        into the heat after dawn meditation.
Above us, insulation foam pushes an eye,
        yellow and spongy,
through the foil ceiling.
The acacias light the valley
smelling of lemonade and cream.
The wind, hot and sour,
is turning east. The gutters
are full. The tank dry.
It is time to get to work.

Multicoloured cereal

1.

The vision sidelined me in the breakfast section
of your local woolies. 9.45pm on a Tuesday,
just wanting to buy peanut butter when,
there she was, the slobbery spawn of our matched
bodies, chewing on an orange segment
in a beachside public park, at least a decade
out of grasp. Woodchips scattered in nearby grass
from the collision-ending of the plastic slide,
that beaming yellow monument. Ants
rushing to collect hundreds and thousands from
the gingham-print picnic blanket, around
the enormous drops of juice plunging
from her chin. And in the vision,
that daughter had a name,
a ghost's name. I can't say it now.

2.

I wanted to ask which part of me
is an ice brick stressing in an open esky
but she adds that visions are different.
Faults in the linoleum and smeared
footprints leading back to a smashed bottle
of chocolate sauce. The shards
laughing out of the sticky mess and I slipped
right there in the middle of the aisle.
The other shoppers pretending to not see.
Boxes upon boxes of multicoloured cereal,
no sympathy.

3.

Every family gathering for the rest of the year
your Uncle Ross goes on about
how we should sue woolies
even though all I got was a mute bruise
summitting thigh to buttocks like a jungle gym.
Even though every millisecond
the beach park playgrounds are melting
a little more out of shape and if I could raise
anything with you it would be hell.
But who would pay the taxes in our old age?
Would make it worth minting
better ways through all this drought?

4.

A month later I snub water restrictions
and lie in a warm bath, wolfing
down parsley, ginger, rosemary,
chalky vitamin C tablets – anything
to make the vision return, lay eyes on the ghost
of our resilience so she can tell me
how the rhyme ends. Look at me
with her cherry cheeks and big brown eyes
and promise some kind of future.
Some kind of escape plan. The rivers
bleed. Turn to mud, then mush, then grit.
It clings like yolk to my thighs
at the water line as I float in wonder
at what unimaginable forms could pull
themselves out of all this waste.

Sausage meat

After work we walk through the thick of it,
under the oxide sculpture bridges emerging
from the smoke to see all the bags of dog shit
blown into the harbour breaking the grimy
surface of the water like aspirations.
And not cry. As if we were pristine
profile corflute signs surrounded by
all this emergency with payday groceries.

The day puts on its long sleeves. The sun
suspended like a glob of flame-red wax
in the lava lamp of air pollution.
Tonight, australia is an election day
sausage with the skin pulled back. Equal parts
doesn't want to know what it's hiding in itself
and can't stop apologising about the curl
of barbecue onion spilled on your shoe.

One friend is preparing to duck walk
in the next suburb over. Another
is wheatpasting coal-dark humour and all
we can talk about is how to turn water
into water. When it feels like we've spent
our very last dollar on breakfast juice.
And we're listing all the ways that art can kill you.
And believing that being human is a team sport
where one side spends everything they have – which is,
in the end, everything – to soak a little longer.

Brood

Glossy and black those chickens sure are spoilt.
Every afternoon you bring out the scraps
to become food for the anonymous dead,
the hens flocking like ravenous mourners.

Every afternoon you bring out the scraps.
Shoes off, shirt unbuttoned, head open.
The hens flocking like ravenous mourners,
flustered through the motions, dusty and grey.

Shoes off, shirt unbuttoned, head open.
You wash the working day from hand and mouth.
Flustered through the motions dusty and grey,
waiting for space in the slaughterhouse line.

You wash the working day from hand and mouth.
Glossy and black those chickens sure are spoilt.
Waiting for space in the slaughterhouse line
to become food for the anonymous dead.

Landscaping for the masses

Everything boxed and bagged and
rammed in the boot and back seat
there is nowhere for the sapling to go
but to wedge the black plastic pot
between your knees and let particles
of soil escape onto the upholstery.
Driving away from the garden centre
and towards somewhere that is not home
you read the tag for the first time:
'drought hardy with pruning' and
'relatively short lived'.
We anticipate the loss.
But there was always something
bold about the purchase.
A hole in which to sow
the belief that we will stop
somewhere long enough to plant
before its little life beats us
to the full four to six metres
espoused by the nursery hand.
Even as we dip our toes into
the darkest projections, keep believing
in somewhere the electricity doesn't
flag so often. Where we can have
a shower curtain that isn't haunted.
And the dormant viruses will stop
escaping from the permafrost.
And the taps will stay on. Even if
all we can keep is one more tree.

Just add water

Written on the land of the Stoney Nakoda, Blackfoot, and Tsuut'ina Nations

1.

I pay good money to lie in a salty bath
of nothing. My favourite thing about
sensory deprivation is how it forces you
to feel all the parts that are hurting. The person
who takes my credit card is australian
and writes poetry. We have 17 mutual friends
on facebook and she gives me a discount.

                       When I get out of the aching
nothingness I am a milked almond.
While drinking the complimentary herbal tea,
the australian asks what I thought about in there.
Awkwardly, the honest answer is her
slipping cleanly into the salt beside me.
But I say, honestly, I just breathed
until I fell asleep the jetlag has been pretty bad
She says cool and gives me her photography
business card and later doesn't email back.

2.

There is so much water here I can't adjust
the shower pressure and 600 people planning
a pipeline. I wade through the flood of their figures
as they take iphone photos of the divine landscape
without losing a breath. I buy a bagel and moan
about it to Cashier Joe and he says that's true
but you know there's been 3 freight train crashes
in the Bow Valley this year alone and people
are just doing their jobs. And we are cowards,
white as paper bags and bearing no witness to
the displacement of ghosts. Later, in my studio
(white sheets, balcony, coffee machine, en suite)
objects do not fly from the tables. But that night
I wake in paralysis surrounded by the idea of people I love.

3.

Back home, my mother collects the discovery
garden packets from woolworths. They accumulate
like bystanders on top of her fridge. Wrapped
in their white shrouds and waiting to sprout
if one would just shake the contents and
add water. That's the thing about
australia[?] – the way the seasons move
around this big dry place we get ~~fresh strawberries~~
bushfires all year round. That's the problem
with australians[?], we don't know
a nightmare even when we see it in the bag
for good. Giving away seed starter kits and
adventures in the great[?] outdoors[?]

4.

I am fissured to learn 'suffer' comes from
to bear from below. That there are coral reefs
at the crowns of these mountains from when they were
seabeds. But no one mentions the bones
unearthed in the renovations. At breakfast
I meet a playwright who tells me every night here
she's dreamt of her dead dog. Of holding
its bloody body until the poor curly thing
went limp. The playwright calls it a big zit
in the psyche finally having the pus squeezed
into the stark light of day. And, my-god,
something is rotten in the state. And something
is surfacing from its grave in the substrate.

5.

Names are stories we tell ourselves and
most of them are inaccurate. The water here
is different to the water there. But all
the water has history. Halfway up the trail
the genius whacks the traction out from under
my boot and my heartbeat won't settle back
into itself. I dribble off the mountainside,
reminded there are some places whose real names
mean you are meant to leave as quickly as you arrive.

ACKNOWLEDGEMENTS

'Spooks' previously appeared in *Cordite Poetry Review*, No. 88 'Transqueer' and *Solid Air* (UQP, 2019)

'The Tower' was commissioned by Red Room Poetry with Wollongong City Council

'Happy Birthday' previously appeared in *Cordite Poetry Review*, No. 87 'Difficult'

'Just Add Water' was written on the land of the Stoney Nakoda, Blackfoot, and Tsuut'ina Nations while in residence at the Banff Centre for Creativity, program undertaken with support from Writing NSW

'Compost' previously appeared in Baby Teeth Journal (April 2019)

ACKNOWLEDGEMENTS

Firstly, many thanks to Dan for all your work creating this book with me, and all the work Subbed In does. Thanks to Linda, Karolina, Alan, and Iona for providing crucial feedback on earlier versions of *In The Drink*. With a hat tip (or queer nod of recognition) to Emma, An, Zoe, Lorin, Melanie, Jesse, Daniel, Kate, David, Andrew and all the poets I've had the pleasure of working with near and far. Thanks to the Creative Writing faculty at UOW, especially Shady Cosgrove and Chrissy Howe.

Much gratitude is owed to all the friends and family held between the covers of this volume, with special acknowledgements to An, Bons, Bruria, Emma, Iona, Karolina, Michaela, and Peter. And thanks to George for the flowers.

In memory of Thomas Martin Crocker.

Big love to William Anthony Crocker.

ABOUT THE AUTHOR

Emily Crocker is a poet, educator, and organiser who now lives, learns, works, and writes in Naarm (Melbourne). Emily's work in all arenas is informed by a politics of queer togetherness and class criticism, developed through lived experience and invaluable community connections. Emily grew up on Dharawal land in outer south-western Sydney, and came of age in Wollongong's spoken word scene. Since then, she has created poetic and performance works with Shopfront Arts Coop and Campbelltown Arts Centre, and has been commissioned by Wollongong Writers Festival, Merrigong Theatre, and Red Room Poetry. Education is central to Emily's practice and she has facilitated workshops in countless schools, youth centres, community places, and libraries. Emily completed a Bachelor of Arts at the University of Wollongong and is currently working towards a Master of Teaching through the University of Melbourne. *In The Drink* is her second collection, following *Girls and Buoyant* (Subbed In, 2017).

ABOUT SUBBED IN

Subbed In is an independent literarararararararary organisation and (very) small publisher. Subbed In programs events and publishes award-winning books that aim to elevate the voices of trans people, people of colour, non-binary people, sex workers, women, people with a disability, LGBTQIA+ people, First Nations people, survivors, working class people, and anyone who finds themselves on the margins of the supremely white, cis, heteronormative, capitalist, colonial, ableist, patriarchal hellscape in which we live. We jam econo.

www.subbed.in

ALSO BY EMILY CROCKER

GIRLS AND BUOYANT

Pinky-promise me you won't die tonight.
You shook my little finger back.
I put the car keys on the bedside anyway
and held your cells, rocking themselves apart,
together until the pharmacy reopened.

~

Emily Crocker complicates home and family in her debut book, *Girls and Buoyant*. With sensitivity and wry observation, Crocker explores old suburbs and new losses at the intersection of late capitalism and queer love.

"Crocker has a vivid way with her imagery, an almost casual ability to draw attention to the unexpected. How can 'the names of the other rocks' move out of someone's 'mind like an abattoir'?"
            - David Dick, *Cordite Poetry Review*

ISBN 9780648147527

Available from www.subbed.in/shop and all good book retailers.

ALSO AVAILABLE FROM SUBBED IN

apocalypse scroll like it was normal
by kenji kinz

Sexy Tales of Paleontology
by Patrick Lenton

*When I die slingshot my ashes
onto the surface of the moon*
by Jennifer Nguyen

blur by the
by Cham Zhi Yi

HAUNT (THE KOOLIE)
by Jason Gray

The Hostage
by Šime Knežević

*If you're sexy and you know
it slap your hams*
by Eloise Grills

wheeze
by Marcus Whale

Parenthetical Bodies
by Alex Gallagher

The Naming
by Aisyah Shah Idil

Girls and Buoyant
by Emily Crocker

Uncle Hercules and other lies
by Patrick Lenton

www.subbed.in

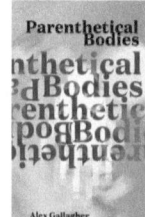

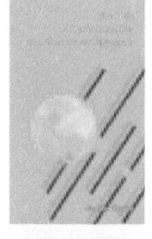

www.ingramcontent.com/pod-product-compliance
Lightning Source LLC
Chambersburg PA
CBHW022019290426
44109CB00015B/1237